Avalanche!

John Rickus

Rosen Classroom Books & Materials
New York

Published in 2003 by The Rosen Publishing Group, Inc.
29 East 21st Street, New York, NY 10010

Copyright © 2003 by The Rosen Publishing Group, Inc.

Book Design: Ron A. Churley

Photo Credits: Cover, p. 1 © John Terence Turner/FPG International; pp. 4–5 © SuperStock; p. 7 © Paul A. Souders/Corbis; pp. 8–9 © Galen Rowell/Corbis; p. 11 © Marc Garanger/Corbis; p. 12 © Peter Southwick/Stock, Boston Inc./ Picture Quest; p. 14 © Phil Miller/Corbis.

ISBN: 0-8239-6380-2
6-pack ISBN: 0-8239-9562-3

Manufactured in the United States of America

Contents

How Snow Forms

Snow is formed when water **vapor** in the air **freezes** and becomes tiny pieces of ice. The pieces come together and form a snowflake. The snowflake grows larger as more and more pieces of ice come together. When the snowflake gets heavy enough, it falls from the sky.

Every snowflake has a different shape.

Layers of Snow

As snow falls, many **layers** build on top of each other. Sun, wind, and how hot or cold it is can change the shape of snowflakes after they hit the ground. These changes may make some layers of snow weaker than other layers. These weak layers will move easily.

There are millions of avalanches all over the world each year.

How an Avalanche Starts

An **avalanche** (AV-uh-lanch) happens when something makes a weak layer of snow move down a mountain. An avalanche can be caused by wind, someone on skis, or even by the sound of someone's voice! Some avalanches are very large. They can knock down trees and houses.

A very large avalanche may have enough snow to fill twenty football fields with snow ten feet deep!

What Is a Sluff?

When new snow falls, it sometimes piles on top of snow that is wet or icy. Sometimes the new snow moves down the mountain. This is called a sluff avalanche. A sluff happens when the weak layer of snow is on top. Sluffs don't carry a lot of snow. The snow they do carry is light and fluffy, like powder.

In a sluff, the snow picks up more snow as it moves. It spreads out in the shape of a big triangle.

Slab Avalanches

A slab avalanche is another kind of avalanche. A slab avalanche happens when the weak layer of snow is deep down. When this weak layer slides, all the snow on top of it slides with it. This snow is strong and hard, and is called a slab. Slab avalanches carry a lot of snow. They are so powerful that they can take trees and huge rocks down the mountain!

 A slab avalanche can move as fast as 200 miles per hour!

Keeping People Safe

People are in danger when they are in an avalanche area. **Experts** do avalanche control to make avalanches happen on purpose.  They remove weak snow and make the area safe for people. They do this late at night or early in the morning, when nobody can get hurt.

Glossary

avalanche   A mass of snow that suddenly slides down the side of a mountain.

expert   Someone who knows a lot about a certain thing.

freeze   To be turned from a liquid into a solid by the cold, such as when water turns to ice.

layer   One thickness of something lying over or under another.

vapor   A liquid that has turned into a gas.

Index